*DAYS OF TRAGEDY*

*The Assassination of a President:*
# ABRAHAM LINCOLN

**Written by:**
**Sue L. Hamilton**

Published by Abdo & Daughters, 6537 Cecilia Circle, Bloomington, Minnesota 55435

Library bound edition distributed by Rockbottom Books, Pentagon Tower, P.O. Box 36036, Minneapolis, Minnesota 55435

Library of Congress Number: 89-084902          ISBN: 0-939179-54-7

Cover Photo by: Bettmann Archive
Inside Photos by: Bettmann Archive

# Edited by: John C. Hamilton

# FORWARD

Laughter filled Ford's Theater the night of April 14, 1865. On stage, the comedy "Our American Cousin" played for a full house, which included special guests, the President and Mrs. Lincoln.

John Wilkes Booth moved unnoticed across the back of the balcony in the Washington, D.C. theater. As a popular actor, he had served the Confederacy not as a Rebel soldier, but as a smuggler. Moving freely back and forth between the North and South with his acting company, he brought medical supplies and ammunition across enemy lines. Still, he had never played a major part in helping his homeland. Eager for fame and skilled as a marksman, Booth had come up with a plan that he believed would make him the hero he always imagined. Dressed in black, he walked like a shadow . . . a shadow of death.

The audience roared with laughter at a particularly funny line in the play. Booth entered the Presidential Box, pointed his gun at the back of Lincoln's head and fired! The president lurched forward in his chair, then arched backwards and slumped down.

A single shot was all Booth needed to make history.

## CHAPTER 1 — KIDNAP LINCOLN

On March 16, 1865, a month before the assassination, popular actor John Wilkes Booth assembled six Confederate friends at a Washington, D.C. boarding house. Tall, muscular Lewis Payne knew how to handle himself. John Surratt, whose widowed mother owned the boarding house they were in and a tavern outside the city, was a devoted Rebel. David Herold, a drug clerk in Washington, would obey any of Booth's orders. George Atzerodt knew the

countryside well and kept a ferryboat on which he transported Southern spies. And lastly, boyhood friends and ex-Confederate soldiers Samuel Arnold and Michael O'Laughlin were also present at the meeting.

"Lincoln is going to a play at Campbell Hospital tomorrow," said Booth to his partners. "Once he's outside the city, we can kidnap him."

Booth's plan was to seize Lincoln and hold him for ransom. "If the North wants their president back, they'll have to end this war," said Booth, his voice rising. "The South will be free to form its own country. A country of white leaders and black slaves! Or, at the very least," he said, lowering his voice to a quiet whisper, "We'll exchange him for several hundred of our captured Southern boys."

The following day each Rebel waited in his assigned position. "How much longer?" asked Payne, shifting uncomfortably on his saddle in the cool March air. "We've been here for hours."

"As long as it takes," said Booth, his ears listening to every sound.

Time passed slowly. Suddenly, they heard it — the sound of horses and a carriage. Quickly they mounted up. It took only minutes for the presidential coach to reach their hiding place at the side of the road.

Seeing no guards, a brief smile crossed Booth's face. However, everyone knew of Lincoln's great strength. Even at the age of 56, it wasn't going to be easy capturing the 6'4" president. "I hope Payne is up to this," thought Booth, depending on his companion's strength to handle Lincoln. Tensely, Booth nudged his horse forward, pistol drawn. The others followed, surrounding the carriage and forcing the driver to stop.

Dismounting, Payne flung open the carriage door and looked inside. Much to his dismay, inside sat Supreme Court Chief Justice Salmon P. Chase. "What is the meaning of this?" asked a confused Chase, who was going to the play in place of the president. Lincoln at that moment was instead presenting a battle flag to the governor of Indiana — right in Booth's own hotel!

"He's not in here!" yelled Payne to Booth.

Rushing over, Booth looked for himself. "Let's get out of here," yelled the young actor. Booth turned and raced away, with the others close behind. After hours of waiting, months of planning, his plot was ruined. He had failed. Worse, the would-be kidnappers now risked being identified and arrested.

The next day, Chief Justice Chase reported the event to Secretary of War Edwin Stanton. Chase, however, could not say who the men were. Stanton, who had often been accused by Lincoln of "worrying too much," used the kidnapping attempt to convince Lincoln that, as president, he must keep guards surrounding him at all times. Lincoln reluctantly agreed.

## CHAPTER 2 — THE WAR IS OVER

"The war is over! Lee surrendered! The war is over!"

It was April 9, 1865, the Sunday before Easter, when General Robert E. Lee surrendered to Union General Ulysses S. Grant. The Rebel capital in Richmond, Virginia had been taken by Union soldiers slightly more than a week before. Confederate President Jefferson Davis and General Lee had tried to gather their forces and strike a unified blow against the Yankees. But as the battle raged, it was clear to General Lee that the time had come for the fighting and dying to stop.

Quietly, in a small courthouse in Appomatox, Virginia, Lee surrendered his small 9,000-man army to General Grant and his 100,000 Union troops. It was an honorable surrender, as President Lincoln had ordered, "With malice towards none, and charity for all."

Back in Washington, the news hit the streets early Monday morning. Yells and cheers filled the air. The war was over! The soldiers would be coming home. Once again, the states were united. Lincoln listened to the excitement from inside the White House. An expression of calm filled his eyes as he said, "The nightmare is finally over."

John Wilkes Booth stood staring at the newspaper headlines. Shocked and horrified, Booth looked up and muttered, "My God, I no longer have a country!"

Booth had always believed he would do one great deed that would change everything for the South. He would be a hero. The man who saved the South. Now that was over. Everything was over. He had nothing left. As cheering, music, and singing filled the streets, Booth walked quietly and sadly home. His world was dead.

## CHAPTER 3 —
## KILL THE PRESIDENT

President Lincoln and the entire city of Washington gathered together on April 14, Good Friday, to welcome General Grant back home. It was a day that would live in history forever.

As the president met with his cabinet and Grant, laughing and joking, another meeting was going on in Surratt's boarding house. "It's not over yet," said Booth to Payne, Atzerodt, and Herold. "The president is going to the theater tonight. I have a plan."

"What's to be done, Booth?" questioned Payne. "The war is over. Ended."

"No, it's not!" snapped Booth, slamming his fist on the table. "If I kill Lincoln, and if you and Herold finish off Secretary of State Seward, while Atzerodt kills Vice President Johnson, the North will be leaderless. General Lee can 'unsurrender,' and the South will rise again!"

Doubtful at first, the three listened to Booth's plans. Excitement filled the young actor's voice as he detailed step-by-step what they were to do. In the end, all agreed that it was possible . . . and that it was their duty as Southerners.

After the meeting, Booth walked over to Ford's Theater. He had spent so much time there acting, his mail was often sent to the theater's address. No one thought twice about Booth's presence, even though it had been well over six months since he had done any acting on that stage.

Walking around the balcony, he came to the door which closed upon the State Box, where the president would sit. It had already been prepared with flags draped over the balcony and a picture of President Washington in the middle. Booth first looked around, and then quietly drilled a hole into the door. This he would use as a peep hole. He knew that once he walked into the State Box, he'd have to kill the president immediately. The peep hole would let him confirm exactly where Lincoln was sitting.

Quickly, Booth finished drilling. Before leaving, he checked to be sure that a wood board was in place behind the door. Some weeks earlier, the door's lock had broken, and the board was wedged between the door and the wall to act as a lock. Booth planned to use this to his advantage that evening.

Everything was set. Booth left to join his friends at the tavern next door. Together, they would share a drink before the evening's activities began.

# CHAPTER 4 — PLEASE, DON'T GO

General Grant spoke quietly and somewhat uncomfortably to President Lincoln as the cabinet meeting concluded. "Sir, Mrs. Grant has asked me to convey our regrets. We cannot attend the theater with you tonight. Mrs. Grant would like to catch the last train for New Jersey, where our children are in school. It has been quite some time since we've seen them."

"Understood," said Lincoln, although disappointed. It was no secret that Mrs. Grant and Mrs. Lincoln did not get along. However, there were other reasons for the declined invitation. Earlier in the day, Secretary of War Stanton had urged Grant to find a reason not to go to the theater with Lincoln. Stanton, still concerned with the president's safety, hoped that Lincoln would also decide not to go to the theater.

However, that was not to be the case. Although tired, Lincoln knew that people were expecting him to attend the play. He made arrangements for New York Senator Harris' daughter, Clara, and her husband-to-be, Major Henry Rathbone, to go in Grant's place.

Stanton made one final attempt at keeping Lincoln from the public appearance when the president requested Major Thomas Eckert to accompany him as his guard.

"Stanton," said Lincoln, "I have seen Eckert break five pokers, one after the other, over his arm, and I am thinking he would be the kind of man to go with me this evening. May I take him?"

"I'm sorry sir, but I cannot spare Eckert tonight," said Stanton, hoping to keep the president from going out. It didn't. Instead, Lincoln assigned John F. Parker, a much-less experienced White House policeman, to accompany him.

# CHAPTER 5 — BOOTH'S REVENGE FOR THE SOUTH

Having picked up their guests, the Lincolns arrived late to the theater. The play had already begun when the president entered the State Box. However, orchestra leader William Withers, Jr. wasn't about to let the president come in unnoticed. Seeing Lincoln's tall, lean form, he stopped the play and led the orchestra in the honorary song, "Hail to the Chief."

The audience rose to its feet, loudly cheering and clapping for several minutes. The serious president was delighted with the warm greeting. A smile filled his worn face as he stood near the edge of the box, bowing with gentle dignity to the happy crowd. He was glad he had come.

Lincoln sat down, and the play, "Our American Cousin," continued. The comedy was entertaining, and Mrs. Lincoln sat with her hand grasping the president's, enjoying every moment. Two hours into the play, about 10:10 p.m., Booth struck.

18

Dressed in black, Booth moved around the back of the balcony to the State Box's door. It was unguarded! John Parker had left his post — perhaps to go next door for a quick drink at the tavern, or possibly to get a better view of the stage. Whatever his reason, he abandoned the president when Parker was needed the most.

As though acting out a play he had written earlier that afternoon, Booth entered the State Box and blocked off the door with the piece of wood. Turning, he paused only a second to peek through the hole he'd drilled in the second door. Beyond the door sat Lincoln on the far left, in his favorite rocking chair. Booth waited for a particularly funny line in the play, then moved quickly into the State Box. As the audience roared with laughter, the killer took several steps forward, raised his single-shot derringer pistol, and fired inches from the back of Lincoln's head.

Lincoln jerked forward, backward, and slumped down. Horror filled the faces of Mrs. Lincoln and her guests. Major Rathbone leaped up to grab Booth, only to be stabbed in his left arm by a hunting knife Booth pulled from his coat.

Below, the audience and actors didn't know what the excitement was. Many believed it was part of the play. However, Mary Lincoln's piercing shriek told them it was something much worse.

Booth suddenly became the center of confused attention as he stood near the edge of the State Box, ready to leap down onto the stage. Looking at the audience, he said in a loud, clear voice, "Sic semper tyrannis!" It was Virginia's state slogan, meaning "Thus always to tyrants."

Rathbone, his coat sleeve drenched with his own blood, leaped forward yelling, "Stop that man!" Booth jumped over the edge, but the spur of his right boot caught on one of the flags. For a brief second, he dangled 11 feet above the stage.

Suddenly, Booth fell. Awkwardly, he landed on the wooden stage. He heard the "snap!" of his left leg breaking, but he had to get away! Before anyone really knew what was happening, the 26-year-old actor-turned-killer hobbled across the stage and escaped out the back, galloping away on a horse he had waiting. His job was done. Revenge!

22

Meanwhile, his other companions had not been quite so successful. George Atzerodt stood outside Vice President Johnson's hotel in the cold April night, rain soaking him. Unlike Booth, he didn't have the nerve to go through with it. Instead of going to Johnson's room, his feet led him to a nearby tavern.

David Herold and Lewis Payne did try to do as Booth had ordered. Herold waited outside, holding the horses, as Payne approached Secretary of State Seward's home. Pretending to have medicine for Seward, who had been in a serious horse and buggy accident nine days earlier, Payne insisted on delivering it only to Seward, and bullied his way in. Eldest son Frederick Seward tried to stop the muscular Payne, only to be beaten senseless with Payne's pistol. Determined, Payne raced into Secretary Seward's room, pausing only to knock out a guard. Quickly he moved over to the bandaged secretary, who was lying helplessly in bed. Payne pulled a knife from his coat and stabbed Seward several times.

Wildly, he turned, shrieking, "I'm mad! I'm mad!" and raced through the house stabbing three other people on his way out.

Outside, Herold heard Seward's daughter Fanny cry out, "Murder! Murder!" Afraid of being caught, he kicked his horse into a fast gallop, leaving Payne to take care of himself.

Payne escaped out the front door, threw his knife in the street, and raced for his horse. He galloped away in the dark, completely lost without Herold.

Inside, Seward looked up at his guard and said, "I am not dead; send for a surgeon, send for the police, close the house." Miraculously, Payne's attack on Seward and his household had not caused even one death.

## CHAPTER 6 — FIND BOOTH

A bullet lodged in his brain, Lincoln lived through the night. His wife, eldest son, and Cabinet members surrounded him. At 7:22 a.m., Saturday, April 15, Abraham Lincoln, 16th President of the

United States, breathed his last breath. Stanton, who had tried so desperately to keep the president from attending the theater, sobbed sadly, "Now he belongs to the ages."

People across the country cried for the loss of one of the wisest and kindest presidents ever. Many had known him as "Father Abraham." He had led the country through four years and 42 days of bloodly civil war. Four million black slaves were freed. The North and South were again united. Now, tragically, his life was ended by one madman's bullet.

The capture of John Wilkes Booth was vital. A reward of $50,000 was offered by the War Department for Booth, and $25,000 for Herold. Once a famous and adored actor, Booth was now a crazed killer, sought after not by adoring audiences, but by soldiers and police.

Booth got away that night, meeting David Herold as planned. They stopped briefly at Surratt's tavern to pick up a rifle and supplies. After changing horses, they rode on. Although stopped by several road guards, Booth used his acting skills to convince the sentries that they were headed for home. He didn't even bother to use a false name, although Herold did. The guards, unaware of the tragic happenings in the city, allowed the killer and his companion to pass.

At 4:00 a.m., crazed with pain from his broken leg, Booth and Herold rode their horses into the yard of Dr. Samuel Mudd. Barely able to walk, Booth hobbled up the steps to the doctor's house, pounding on the door until Mudd came down. Dr. Mudd placed the leg between two thin pieces of wood, making a splint that would hold the leg steady. The doctor let Booth and Herold sleep in his house. As Booth rested comfortably, the president died in a small boarding house across from the theater.

That afternoon, as Andrew Johnson was sworn in as new president of the United States, Booth and Herold rode south. For more than a week, the two hid in a cold, wet swamp. Union troops blanketed the area, and the two were unable to move on.

Finally, their chance came. They continued south, crossing the Potomac River into Virginia, and stopped at a farm owned by Richard Garrett. There, from leads given by local citizens, the troops cornered Booth in Garrett's tobacco barn at 2:00 a.m. on April 26, 1865.

"Come out now!" yelled Lt. Luther Baker, a detective with the troops.

"No!" yelled back Booth. However, the presidential killer offered to come out if he was allowed to come out shooting. An honorable death for himself.

"No!" responded Lt. Baker.

"Well, my brave boys, prepare a stretcher for me," said Booth, figuring that they'd have to kill him before he'd surrender.

At this point, Herold lost his nerve and shouted, "Let me out!"

Booth turned to his companion and yelled, "You coward! Go! Go! I would not have you stay with me!" Herold opened the barn's door and walked out. Immediately, he was grabbed and handcuffed.

After Herold surrendered, Col. Everton Conger, another detective, set fire to the back of the barn, hoping to smoke Booth out. The barn went up in flames. Alone, trapped, and on crutches, Booth turned and moved toward the open barn doors, clearly deciding to surrender. Lt. Baker moved up to arrest the murderer when suddenly, a single shot rang out. Booth went down.

Baker and Conger looked at each other and asked, "Did you fire?" Each responded, "No."

"Who fired?" questioned the two angry detectives, turning to look at the troops. They had wanted to take Booth alive.

"I did," said Boston Corbett, ranking sergeant of the patrol. Known to have done many odd things, officers had felt Corbett was too unstable to take part in Lincoln's funeral parade. Thus left behind, he had been assigned this duty. Corbett believed that Booth was aiming his gun at him, and decided to get Booth before Booth could get him.

Booth, shot in the neck, although not yet dead, was pulled from the burning barn by Baker and Conger. Booth turned to Conger and whispered, "Tell mother I died for my country."

Too weak to be moved, the 26-year-old killer lived in great pain for two more hours. He died lying on the cold ground by the smoldering ruins of Garrett's barn. He would never be remembered as a handsome actor. Instead, his last moments on stage would brand him as John Wilkes Booth: the man who killed Abraham Lincoln.

## CHAPTER 7 —
## BOOTH'S "FRIENDS"

Booth's Rebel friends did not escape punishment. David Herold, Lewis Payne, George Atzerodt, and Mrs. Mary E. Surratt were captured, tried and found guilty. All four were hanged on July 7, 1865.

Mrs. Surratt was later found to have no real part in the president's killing, other than it was at her boarding house that the plans were made. She was the first woman in U.S. history to be hanged.

Her son, John Surratt, escaped the country, and was not found until November 1866. His mother's sad death aided him in his own trial. In 1868, charges were dropped, and John Surratt went free.

Dr. Samuel Mudd, Samuel Arnold, and Michael O'Laughlin were sent to prison. Mudd and Arnold were released in 1869. O'Laughlin died in 1867 of yellow fever while still in prison.

So ended Booth and his friends' "glorious" attempt to save the South. As he had written of Lincoln in his diary, "Our country owned all her trouble to him, and God simply made me the instrument of his punishment." But instead of helping the South, he killed the one man who might have made the post-war years easier. The kind, sensible leader who believed in "charity for all."

# SOURCES CONSULTED

Hanchett, William. **The Lincoln Conspiracies**. Urbana and Chicago: University of Illinois Press, 1983.

Holzer, Harold. "Ford's Theatre," **American History Illustrated**, February 1986, pg. 12-19, 8.

Hunter, Marjorie. "Retracing the Flight of Lincoln's Assassin." **The New York Times**, April 13, 1985.

Irwin, Don. "Book Connects Booth to Rebel Plot." **The Los Angeles Times**, July 30, 1988.

Jordan, Robert Paul. **The Civil War**. Washington, D.C.: National Geographic Society, 1969.

Lattimer, John K. **Kennedy and Lincoln**. New York and London: Harcourt Brace Jovanovich, 1980.

Mercer, Charles. "The Murder of Abraham Lincoln," **Boy's Life**, February 1985, pp. 32, 34, 68.

Reck, W. Emerson. **A. Lincoln: His Last 24 Hours**. Jefferson, North Carolina and London: McFarland & Company, Inc., 1987.

Starkey, Larry. **Wilkes Booth Came To Washington**. New York: Random House. 1976.

Wallechinsky, David, and Wallace, Irving. **The People's Almanac**. New York: Doubleday & Company, Inc., 1975.

Wallechinsky, David, and Wallace, Irving. **The People's Almanac #2**. New York: Doubleday & Company, Inc., 1978.